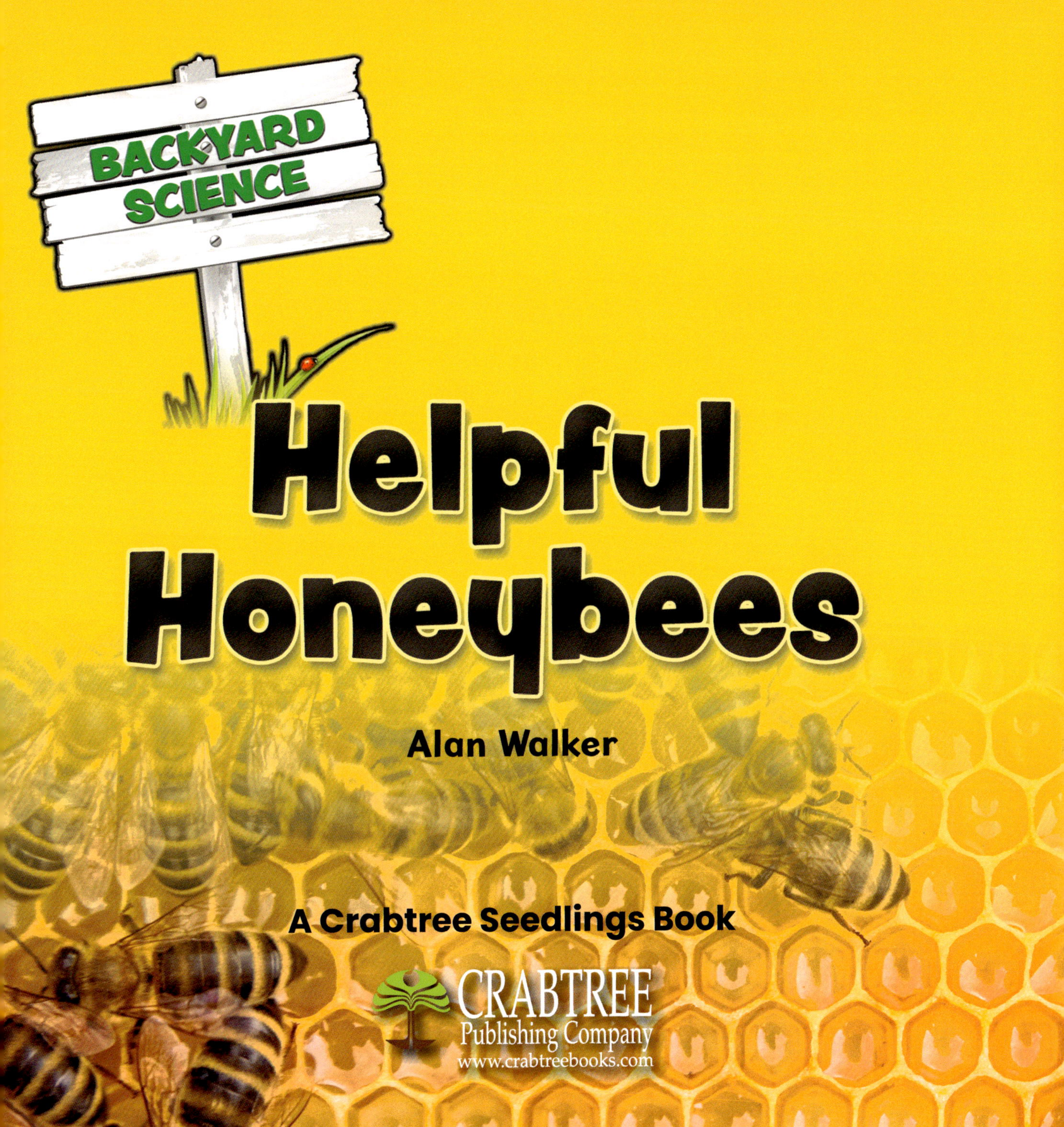

Helpful Honeybees

Alan Walker

A Crabtree Seedlings Book

CRABTREE
Publishing Company
www.crabtreebooks.com

Table of Contents

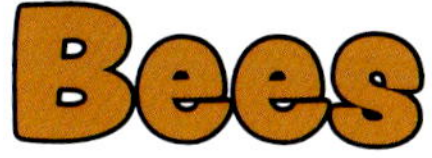

Bees

There are thousands of different kinds of flying insects—one kind is the bee.

There are about 20,000 kinds of bees. The four kinds we may see the most are honeybees, bumblebees, carpenter bees, and sweat bees.

honeybee

bumblebee

carpenter bee

sweat bee

Honeybees

One very important kind of bee is the honeybee. Honeybees are **social** insects that live in **colonies**.

Bee Facts!

Bee colonies can be found anywhere—including inside buildings and trees.

These colonies build homes called hives. Inside the hive, the bees build a comb made of beeswax.

A comb looks like many hexagons.

Three kinds of honeybees live in a hive: a queen bee, drone bees, and worker bees. Each kind has a special job.

Bee Facts!

Queen bee: There is only one queen bee in a hive. Her job is to lay eggs.

Drone bee: Drone bees are male. Their job is to **mate** with the queen.

Worker bee: Worker bees are female. Most of the bees in the colony are worker bees. Worker bees build the hive and comb and collect pollen and **nectar**.

Honeybee Body Parts

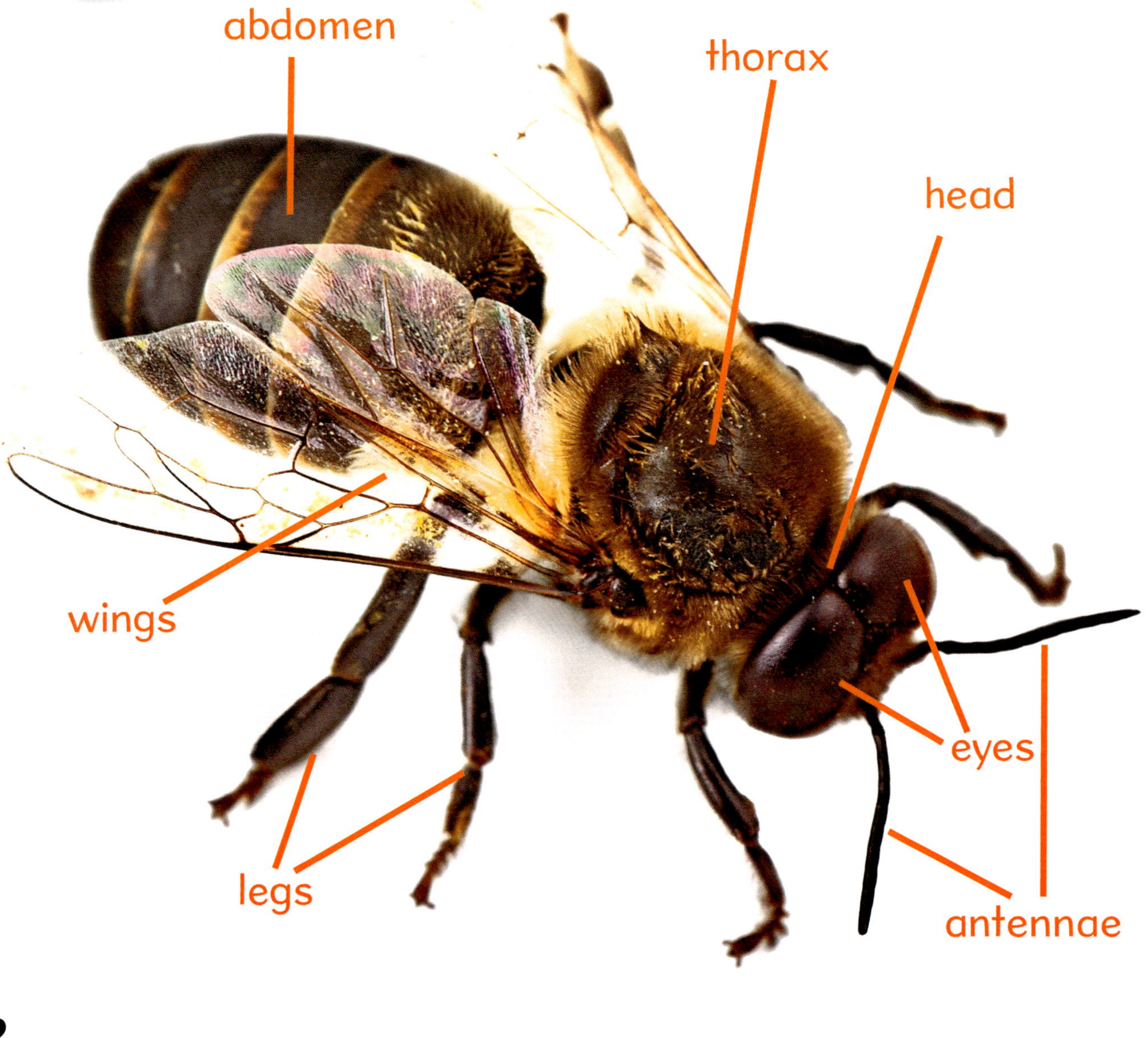

Honeybees have three main body parts: a head, thorax, and abdomen. They also have six legs. This makes them insects.

Some pollen looks like yellow dust.

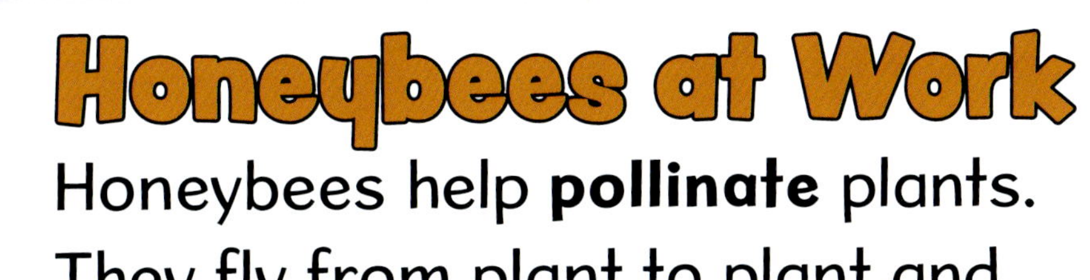

Honeybees at Work

Honeybees help **pollinate** plants. They fly from plant to plant and collect pollen. They carry the pollen on their legs in pollen sacs.

pollen sac

Honeybees also collect nectar. They use their **proboscis** to suck nectar from the flower.

Honeybees store the nectar and pollen in the comb. They turn the nectar into honey. The honeybees use the honey and the pollen for food.

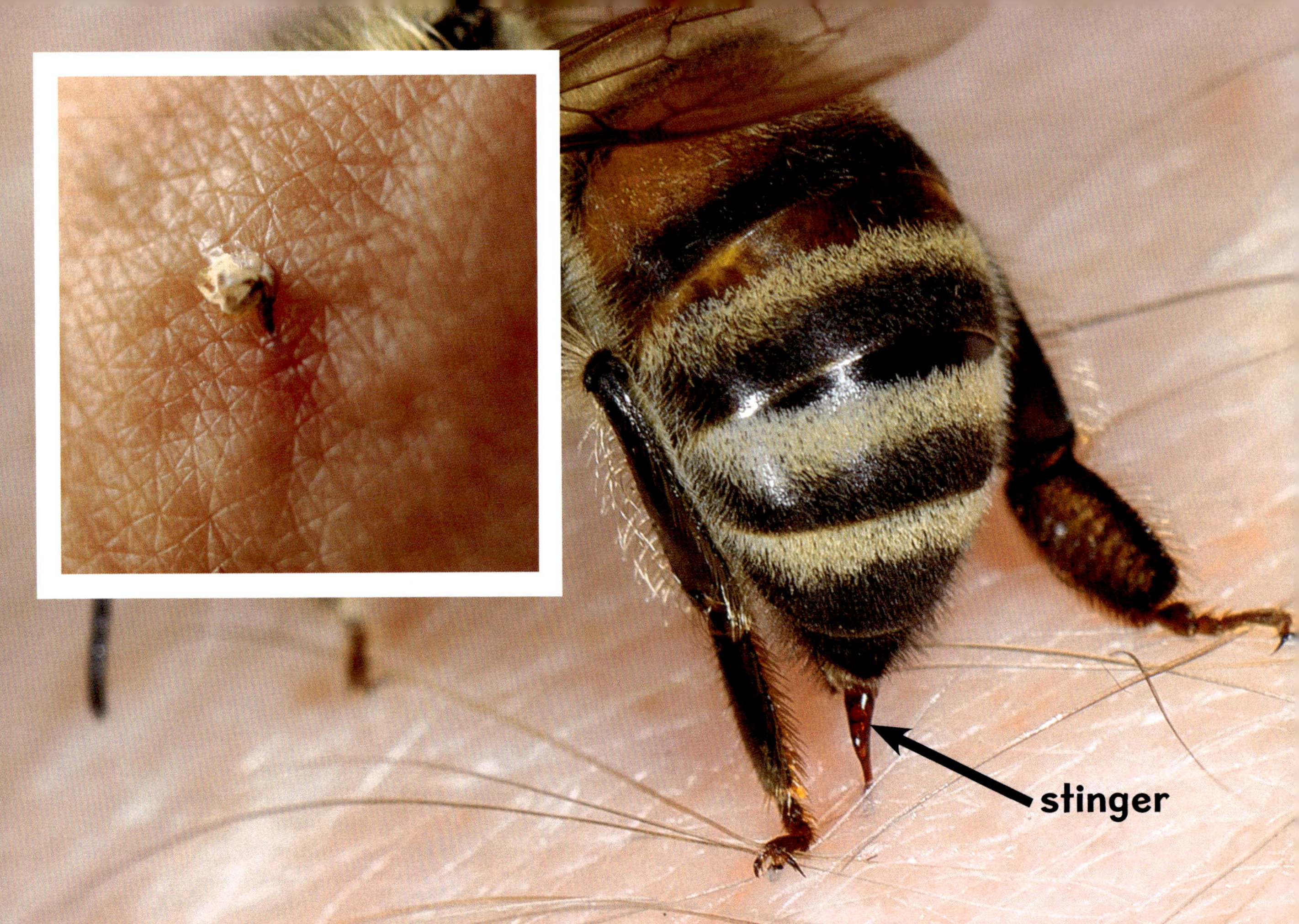

Ouch!

Only female honeybees have a stinger. The stinger is used if the honeybee or colony feels threatened. The sting of a honeybee is painful.

Bee Facts!

When a honeybee stings, its stinger gets pulled from its body. This kills the honeybee.

Honeybees play a very important role in nature. If you see a honeybee, don't be afraid. Don't bother it and it won't bother you.

Glossary

colonies (KOL-uh-neez): Colonies are large groups of animals that live together, such as a colony of bees.

mate (MATE): To mate is to join together for breeding. Drone bees mate with the queen bee.

nectar (NEK-tur): Nectar is a sweet liquid that bees collect from flowers.

pollinate (POL-uh-nate): To pollinate is to transfer pollen from one plant to another. This helps plants produce seeds.

proboscis (pruh-BAHS-is): A proboscis is an animal's long snout or feeding tube.

social (SOH-shuhl): Social animals, such as bees, like to live in groups.

Index

School-to-Home Support for Caregivers and Teachers

This book helps children grow by letting them practice reading. Here are a few guiding questions to help the reader build his or her comprehension skills. Possible answers appear here in red.

Before Reading

- **What do I think this book is about?** I think this book is about honeybees and how they make honey. I think this book is about how very important bees are to the pollinating of plants.
- **What do I want to learn about this topic?** I want to learn more about how honeybees make honey and the comb. I want to learn why bees sting people.

During Reading

- **I wonder why...** I wonder why the female bees do all the hard work. I wonder why there's only one queen bee in each colony.
- **What have I learned so far?** I have learned that only female honeybees sting people. I have learned that when a honeybee stings a person its stinger gets pulled from its body and then the honeybee dies.

After Reading

- **What details did I learn about this topic?** I have learned that there are about 20,000 kinds of bees. I have learned that honeybees fly from plant to plant and collect pollen to leave on other plants.
- **Read the book again and look for the glossary words.** I see the word *colonies* on page 8, and the word *nectar* on page 11. The other glossary words are found on pages 22 and 23.

Library and Archives Canada Cataloguing in Publication

CIP available at Library and Archives Canada

Library of Congress Cataloging-in-Publication Data

CIP available at Library of Congress

Crabtree Publishing Company
www.crabtreebooks.com 1–800–387–7650

Print book version produced jointly with Blue Door Education in 2022

PHOTO CREDITS:
istock.com, shutterstock.com, Cover; a8096b40_190, MariaTkach. PAGE2-3: Jag_cz. PAGE4-5; Ale-ks, K_Thalhofer. PAGE6-7: Oregon DOA_www.oregon.gov ODA, Perboge, akiyoko, Ihor-photograf, defun. PAGE8-9: OlyaSolodenko, Diyana Dimitrova, fpwing. PAGE10-11: Inventori, Kuttelvaserova Stuchelova. PAGE12-13: artisteer, GUHL. PG14-15; LightShaper, Dimijana. PG16-17; ulkas, Pakhnyushchy. PG18-19; balwan. DiyanaDimitrova. PG20-21; Mirko Graul, plew koonyosying, Musat, balwan. Pg22-23: OlyaSolodenko.

Written by: Alan Walker
Production coordinator and Prepress technician: Tammy McGarr
Print coordinator: Katherine Berti

Printed in Canada/122022/CPC20221214

Published in the United States
Crabtree Publishing
347 Fifth Ave.
Suite 1402-145
New York, NY 10016

Published in Canada
Crabtree Publishing
616 Welland Ave.
St. Catharines, Ontario
L2M 5V6